THE COLOUR
VESPA
FAMILY ALBUM

This book is dedicated to David & Eli Gardner, as a token of our love and friendship.

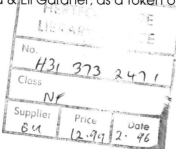

Other books of interest to enthusiasts available from Veloce -

• **Colour Family Album titles** •
Citroën 2CV: The Colour Family Album by Andrea & David Sparrow
Citroën DS: The Colour Family Album by Andrea & David Sparrow
Bubblecars & Microcars: The Colour Family Album by Andrea & David Sparrow

• **Other titles** •
Alfa Romeo. How to Power Tune Alfa Romeo Twin Cam Engines by Jim Kartalamakis
Alfa Romeo Modello 8C 2300 by Angela Cherrett
Alfa Romeo Giulia Coupé GT & GTA by John Tipler
Alfa Romeo Owner's Bible by Pat Braden
Biggles! - The Life Story of Captain W. E. Johns by Peter Berresford Ellis & Jennifer Schofield
Bugatti 46 & 50 - The Big Bugattis by Barrie Price
Bugatti 57 - The Last French Bugatti by Barrie Price
Car Bodywork & Interior: Care & Repair by David Pollard
Cobra - The Real Thing! by Trevor Legate
Completely Morgan - Four Wheelers 1936-68 by Ken Hill
Daimler SP250 (Dart) V-8 by Brian Long
Fiat & Abarth 124 Spider & Coupé by John Tipler
Fiat & Abarth 500 & 600 by Malcolm Bobbitt
Karmann Ghia Volkswagens by Malcolm Bobbitt
Lola T70 by John Starkey
Making MGs by John Price Williams
Mazda MX5/Miata Enthusiast's Workshop Manual by Rod Grainger & Pete Shoemark
MGB. How To Give Your MGB V-8 Power by Roger Williams
Mini Cooper - The Real Thing! by John Tipler
Motorcycling in the '50s by Jeff Clew
Nuvolari: When Nuvolari Raced ... by Valerio Moretti
Pass The MoT by David Pollard
Rover P4 by Malcolm Bobbitt
Triumph TR6 by William Kimberley

First published in 1995 by Veloce Publishing Plc., Godmanstone, Dorset DT2 7AE, England. Fax 01300 341065

ISBN 1 874105 48 0

Readers with ideas for automotive books, or books on other transport or related hobby subjects, are invited to write to the editorial director of Veloce Publishing at the above address.

British Library Cataloguing in Publication Data -
A catalogue record for this book is available from the British Library.

Typesetting (Avant Garde), design and page make-up all by Veloce on Apple Mac.

Printed in Hong Kong

ANDREA & DAVID SPARROW

VELOCE PUBLISHING PLC
PUBLISHERS OF FINE AUTOMOTIVE BOOKS

THANKS

Our grateful thanks to the following:

Clive Mills, Christa Sollbach & Piero Pagnagnelli - International Federation of Vespa Clubs, Yves & Marie-Pierre Le Sellin - Vespa Club France, Charles Caswell - Vespa Club of Britain, Giuseppe Tranchina & Shirley Pattison - Piaggio UK, Snr Burgos - MotoVespa SA, Oliver Körber, Hans Kruger, Kees Portanje, Jac Janssens, Willem Hacken, Norrie Kerr, Patrick Pellen, Jos & Jeanine Janssens, Jan van Pey, Elvira Porqueras, Luis Azcue, Luis Casedemont.

Michael Espenschied, Ralf Kalker, Frank Krämer, Gerd Krämer, Timo Müsil, Ulf-Rüdiger Scholz, Monika Simon, Sascha Weidler, Steffi Zahler,

Heidi Schefe, Maurice Jessen, Joeri & Cindy Janck, Manfred Meier, Mark Green, Davis Sharp, Paul Golding, Barry Baker, Rob Currie, Steve Moore, Jim McCabe, Glen Allen, Steve Langton, Ingrid Bell, Brian Edwards, Robin Rother, Brian Forde.

Carlo Ruggeri, Richard Meissonnier, Antonio Torres,

Eric Djiane-Alegria, Eric Dutra, Joan Ribera Herdes, Juan Navaro, William Rondeler & Heidi, Tillman Siebott, Inge

Priester, Kerstin Bürgel, Domenico Palazzetti, Didier Bongiouanni, Stefan Peruzzi, Adrian Burridge, Bill Drake, Angie Kind, Claudia Smissaert, Candy van der Lans, Manfred Theis, Melanie Junker, Herbert Moroz, Emil Westphal.

Manfred Meesen, Sybille Monnier, Steve Forster, Mark Forster, Tracey Hole, Daniel Divers, Marco Kuhl, Thierry Bijiaoui, François Fantauzzo, Romain Vernet, Benjimin Giuigiue, Cedric Biancone, Ella, Emma Sparrow, Jade Bond, Daniel Icard, Hervè Chouchana, Sharon Whittle, Stan Roukens & Centrum Beeldente Kunst, Sittard, Helen Farley, Pierre Delliere, Robin Davy.

CONTENT

INTRODUCTION

Piaggio's amazingly popular Vespa contributed to a completely changed postwar lifestyle in its home country of Italy. Manufactured under licence in countries around the world and exported in various forms from Italy, Vespa machines - particularly the scooter - have earned a special place in the history of personal transport and in the affections of many past and present owners.

The Vespa has been around for half a century. It first earned its popularity in the austere postwar forties and fifties, evolved to meet the needs of the younger rider in the sixties and changed its style for the late seventies and the eighties. Now new technology has propelled it into the nineties.

The Vespa family also includes the APE commercial in its many forms and the tiny Vespa 400 car, both of which have chapters, and followers, of their own within the Vespa story.

The Vespa is more than just an evolving machine - it is, for many, a passion and a way of life and will continue to be so while Vespas, old or young, remain on the roads of the world.

Andrea Sparrow

THE BIG IDEA

1

The second World War wreaked almost total destruction upon the face of industry in Italy, as elsewhere in Europe. Normal production of peacetime commodities had ended when the demand for munitions became paramount. Factories had been targeted by bombs and often severely damaged, usually beyond economic repair. Workforces had been torn apart, and dreams shattered. Clearly, it was going to be only those of truly entrepreneurial spirit whose businesses would rise from the ashes now that peace had come.

Enrico Piaggio was one such man. In 1938, Piaggio had inherited two factories in Tuscany from his father and now, seven years on, they were in ruins. Fortunately, Piaggio had also inherited his father's business acumen and innovative skills, so he knew what was required. He would have to create a product to fill a real postwar need so that a ready market would be found; a product with a reasonable price tag and, with neither time nor money to retrain the workforce, a product that could be manufac-tured with the skills and equipment they already possessed. No time for lengthy research and development either - he needed brilliant, innovative engineering so that the product would be right from the start.

The Piaggio family businesses had always been concerned with transport of one type or another. Back in 1894, Rinaldo Piaggio had developed his father's humble sawmill into a world-renowned naval fitters, employing master carpenters and joiners, and working for all the best shipyards. In the early years of the century, Piaggio diversified first into railway carriages and then into commercial vehicles of all kinds. By the twenties, he was also producing boats and aeroplanes - he was a pioneer in the field of aircraft for passenger travel, rather than just for military and cargo-carrying purposes. Given the family background, it was not surprising that Enrico fixed upon a method of transport as the answer to his problem of what to build.

The idea that caught Piaggio's imagination was not entirely new. Scooters had

D'Ascanio designed a new two-stroke engine especially for the Vespa.

been attempted before, but without any real success. Piaggio was convinced that a new approach was called for; not a motorcycle/bicycle crossbreed with the advantages of neither and the problems of both, but a real answer to a real problem. For cheap, personal transport was a very big problem for many ordinary Italians at the time. Piaggio discussed his intentions with Corradino D'Ascanio, a brilliant engineer in whom he had great confidence.

The concept that Piaggio described to D'Ascanio was very specific; a woman must be just as comfortable riding the scooter as a man, there must be protection for the rider to prevent splashing in wet weather and clothes damage from leaking oil. There must be a spare wheel, and the whole thing must be light and easy to ride and handle. It must also be inexpensive to buy and maintain. The fulfilment of this concept was to be the Vespa.

The first prototype was put together from whatever parts were available, earning it the nickname *Paperino*- the Italian name for Donald Duck. Piaggio was encouraged enough by the concept prototype to give the go-ahead for the project proper to get underway.

The drawing-board stage for the scooter lasted just five

The Vespa's broad front face was no mere styling exercise - there were to be no splashed legs or spoiled clothing for Vespa riders - and Piaggio insisted in his brief to designer D'Ascanio that the new scooter should be comfortable and practical for women to ride. The earliest Vespas used a system of rods to operate the gearbox - and so later became known as 'Rod' models.

months. So highly tuned was D'Ascanio's vision as an engineer - fifteen years earlier he had built the first really controllable helicopter - that he was able, in a very short space of time, to conquer the majority of the technical problems that occurred. Logistical problems overcome, a few prototype units powered by Sachs engines were

The Vespa brightened the lives of many woman - its sheer usability offered real freedom to travel and socialise.

The Vespa was used by postal authorities in several countries though, unfortunately, not in Britain where the small BSA Bantam motorcycle usually played that particular role.

soon being tested and, by April 1946, the first scooters, now driven by D'Ascanio's specially designed two-stroke engine, were ready to be presented to the Press.

D'Ascanio's elegant design utilised the very skills that were available from the Piaggio workforce. The machine's pressed steel 'body' was a light but sturdy frame supporting and containing all the mechanical parts and, at the same time, providing protection for the rider's legs and clothing. The front wheel was connected by means of a single shaft to the handle-bars; its single sided fork making wheel-changing an easily-managed affair. The 98cc engine, which ran on a 5 per cent two-stroke fuel mixture, was cooled by a forced air system. It was set beside and to the right of the rear wheel, to which it was linked directly. D'Ascanio believed that a chain or universal joint system would be an unnecessary complication; the remit was simplicity in all things. There were three gears; communication with the handlebar left handgrip gearchange being via a system of transmission rods - D'Ascanio disliked the pedal changes used by most motorcycles.

The scooter weighed in at 175lb, and had a maximum speed of 45mph, with a more usual average of around

This and previous page: city winebar or country vinyard - the Vespa's equally at home.

30mph on normal roads. It was cheap to run - over 100 miles to the gallon of fuel. It was not too expensive to produce, and so would be within reach of the man in the *strada*.

The scooter that fulfilled Piaggio's dream was different from anything that had gone before. As well as real practical advantages, it also had a definite character, and consequently was in need of a suitable name. The bulbous rear end, pinched 'waist' and front 'wings', together with the buzzing of the two-stroke engine, suggested a wasp, and so the name *Vespa* was coined.

The Vespa was destined to be an instrument of change; the great freedom and flexibility that it offered were new experiences to many owners in the early days. It was possible to work some distance from your home and commute by Vespa. The radius of your social circle widened overnight. You could pile your children onto a Vespa and head for the seaside. It was possible to look further afield at last. From the ruins of Enrico Piaggio's Pontedera factory had sprung a unique phenomenon.

Not so solemn: Vespa outside the cathedral in Gerona.

The advantages of the Vespa lifestyle were brought to younger riders by the introduction of the 50cc machine.

Opposite: There are countless ways to decorate your Vespa - with, for example, mirrors and flags like this French one.

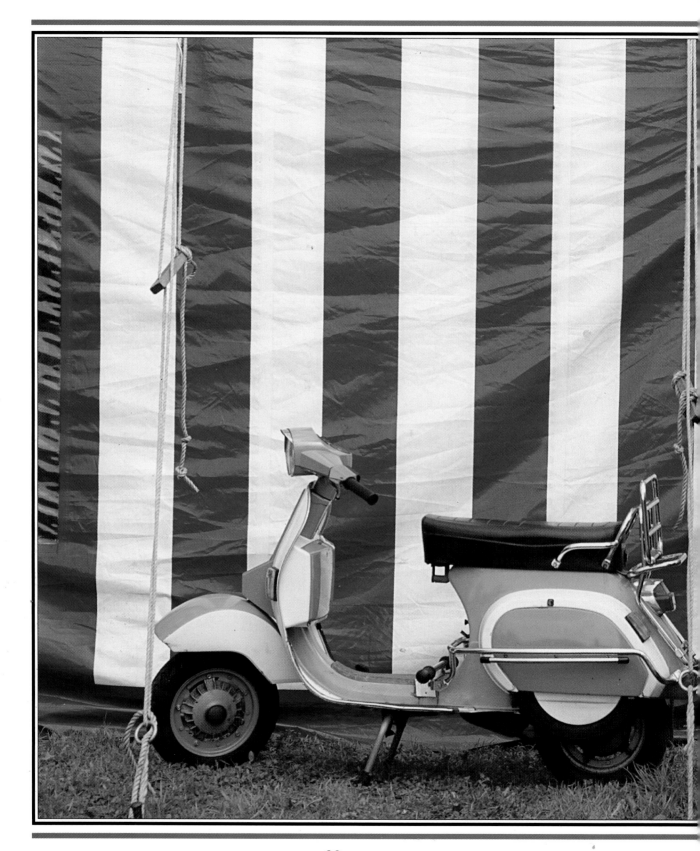

Whichever country they are from, Vespa owners form a strong attachment to their scooters as they travel together.

A German Vespa with lots of chrome, more chrome and, naturlich, flags.

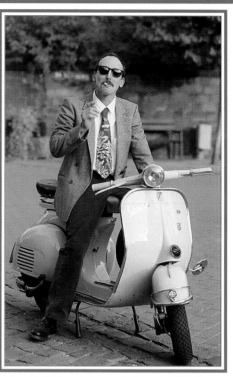

Whether just socialising or dressed for business, the Vespa's still a great way to travel - perhaps to a pizzeria like this where American style meets Italian style.

THE FIRST FIFTY YEARS

By the end of 1945, the stage was set for the introduction of Piaggio's new scooter. The Model V.98 went into production in April 1946. An immediate hit in Italy, the scooter fulfilled all that Piaggio had asked of it and offered the opportunity of a complete change of lifestyle for the ordinary would-be motorist who could not hope to afford a car in the austere postwar conditions. The Vespa was described in the press as "a little two-wheeled car" - not in size or capacity perhaps, but certainly in the flexibility of use that it offered its buyers.

In the first two years of production, over 50,000 Vespa scooters were built - the Vespa phenomenon had begun!

By 1948, the 125 had evolved. With extra power and minor improvements (to the suspension for example), it represented the first step on a long road that would bring Vespas with diverse characteristics - the powerful and sporty Rally 200, the gentle 50 for the young market, the classic new-line look of the late seventies, the futuristic Hexagon of the nineties, the ever-popular GS, the distinctly odd-ball military Vespa, the three wheels of the APE and the four wheels of the Vespa 400.

By the time the 1950s arrived, the worst after-effects of the war years were over for the majority of people and life was returning to normality - albeit a different life to that of prewar days. The Vespa was making its mark, both as cheap transport - which had been Piaggio's intention - and as an object of desire in itself. Vespa clubs were springing up, meetings were being organised and rallies run.

The Vespa 125 of 1951 did away with the rods operating brake, clutch and gear selection in favour of flexible cables. Two years later, the headlamp moved up from the front wing to the handlebars. 1954 brought the first 150, followed two years later by the 150GS: the first sporty Vespa, and destined to be one of the most popular models in its several incarnations.

In the first ten years of production, more than one million Vespas rolled off the production line at Pontedera.

Fifty years before the Vespa, Enrico Piaggio's father had been in the business of providing top-quality fittings and furnishing for ships.

The first Vespa had no stand, instead it was supplied with a small cupped dome to rest on the pavement. The handlebar mounted controls were connected to the appropriate components by rod linkages.

By 1952 the rod linkages of the controls had been replaced by cables and a stand was fitted - this Vespa, though manufactured in Italy, was imported new into Spain.

Another 1952 Spanish resident of Italian origins. Most Vespas of the time were painted green or grey.

A Spanish-built 125 from 1960, the year in which production of the Vespa scooter passed the two million mark.

In Italy alone there were 4000 outlets dedicated to the selling and servicing of Vespas, 8000 spread across the rest of Europe, and another 2000 elsewhere in the world. The Vespa was the scooter market's top seller in more than 100 countries.

The last two years of the 1950s brought restyling for the 125 and 150, with the headlamp integrated into the handlebars and a slightly sleeker profile. The Vespa's popularity was still huge - the two-millionth unit was produced during 1960. Two years later, the GS was presented with a 160cc engine, uprated in 1964 to 180cc.

An important new chapter in the Vespa story opened in 1963 with the introduction of the Vespa 50. This scooter was able to be classified as a

Opposite: The Vespa 50. This model made the advantages of scooter ownership available to 14 year olds in many countries, often without test or licence requirements.

moped and could therefore - at least in its home country - be ridden by anyone of four-

150GS from 1960 shows headlamp integrated into the handlebar unit.

have pedals fitted for moped classification, resulting in a less than elegant hybrid. The 50 was the first Vespa to have its engine's single cylinder inclined at 45 degrees rather than horizontal. A 90cc version of the same basic design would follow. The Vespa 50 was designed by D'Ascanio: however, it was to be the last project he worked on together with Enrico Piaggio, who died in October 1965.

The 50 Super Sprint and 90 Super Sprint models that appeared in 1965 had all the feel of 'Special Edition' Vespas. The narrower front face and handlebars, a 'glovebox' over the centre-mounted spare wheel and chromed silencer gave these Sprint models a sporty look: they were available in red, blue or white. There was a 'new-look' 125, too, the *Primavera*.

1968 brought the 180 Rally - the last incarnation in the GS series which would stay in production until 1973: a lifespan of eighteen years.

teen or over without the need for a driving test or licence. The popularity of the little Vespa was in no doubt on its home ground, where a new market comprising many thousands of young people was ready and waiting. Things were not quite so simple in other countries; in France, for example, it was necessary to

After its launch in 1965, the 90 Super Sprint was sometimes mistakenly described as having a fuel tank over the central spare wheel - in fact it's a luggage box.

Opposite: More kudos than an ordinary moped - and this particular 50 Special has been repainted in a wonderful rosa colour.

The Rally 200, above, was the first Vespa to feature electronic ignition.

The seventies began with the introduction of the Vespa 50 Elestart which, as you've probably guessed, featured an electric starter. More innovation followed two years later with the advent of the Rally 200, the first Vespa with electronic ignition.

Then, in 1977, came an important new development; the 'new line' scooters, with redesigned slimmer styling and improvements to the suspension and shock absorbers. First came the PX series beginning with the 125 and 200: the 150 appearing the following year

The 125 Primavera gave a new look to the oldest model - Vespa 125s had been around, in various forms, for thirty years when the new model was launched.

and an 80 version in 1980. 1982 brought the PK series; basically the same mechanically, but smaller and more compact in size, in 50, 80, 100 and 125 versions. These were followed by *Arcobaleno* (Rainbow) versions and *Automatica* - the first automatic Vespa, which was to lead the way for the future. A sporty version of the 125 in the PX series - the T5 - arrived in 1985.

Two years later, a new scooter was unveiled by Piaggio, the *Cosa*. Aerodynamically styled and tested with the benefit of a wind-tunnel, *Cosa* was produced in 125, 150 and 200 versions. With the *Cosa* model, the Vespa name was being quietly dropped in favour of Piaggio-branding. This has not been easily accepted; in Germany in particular there has been a successful attempt to bring back the Vespa badging alongside that of Piaggio on the modern scooters - these new models may be a new breed, but their heritage is not forgotten

The 1990s brought a new generation of Piaggio scooter for a new generation of scooterists. The *Sfera* was the first of this new breed, which also includes Zip, Quartz and Typhoon, Storm and Skipper. These new scooters have tubular-steel frames, courtesy of computer-aided design, replacing the traditional Vespa load-bearing shell. The bodies of these machines are formed from high-tech plastics

The 90cc Vespa which was based on the 50cc model. It was not the most popular of Vespas so those remaining today are much sought-after.

The 'new line' scooters arrived in the late seventies. This professionally airbrushed PX200E from 1985 turns a few heads.

which are light and easily moulded into aerodynamic shapes in the factory - but less easily deformed on the road. The new-style Piaggio scooter is automatic and easy to drive.

As the fiftieth anniversary of the Vespa approached, Piaggio's flagship scooter, the Hexagon, presented a very different face to the world from the Vespas of old. Its futuristic bodyline, which incorporates a large luggage space, was designed to appeal to a wide market.

The future will of course be influenced by ever-improving technology and fashion; however, while today's new scooterists would not tolerate the technology of twenty-five, let alone fifty years ago, nostalgia never goes out of fashion!

Of all the Vespas, the GS is perhaps the most enduring and popular - the classic scooter.

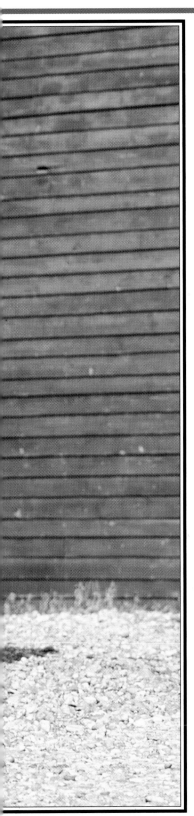

The Cosa was the first scooter to abandon the Vespa name in favour of the Piaggio badge.

There is an environmentally-friendly version of the Zip model with two power units; normal for getting to town, and electric for use when there.

Despite dramatic differences to their forebears, riding the Sfera and Typhoon still creates the same kind of enthusiasm that the older models engendered.

Half a century away from the conception of the 'little two-wheeled car,' the Hexagon - its name alluding to the Piaggio badge shape - is billed as an alternative to motorbike and car.

The Skipper comes in three engine sizes, 80cc 125cc and 150cc, with the option of a catalyser unit to reduce harmful exhaust emissions. Inset: automatic and convenient; the new breed of Piaggio scooters feature simple 'switch on and go' operation.

AROUND THE WORLD

Vespa in the UK

The idea that became the Vespa grew out of Enrico Piaggio's need to relaunch his war-shattered business; the Vespa's arrival in the UK stemmed from a similar need.

The year was 1948: Claude McCormack was on holiday in Italy, but with work very much on his mind. He had recently been appointed Managing Director of motorcycle manufacturer Douglas (Kingswood) Ltd., which was in financial trouble and in the hands of the Official Receiver at the time. Like Piaggio, McCormack knew the strengths of his Bristol-based workforce, and he knew how essential it was to find a speedy solution to the company's immediate postwar problems.

When McCormack spotted his first Vespa he was at first intrigued, then inspired, then convinced - Douglas should build Vespas for the UK. In Britain, Vespas first appeared at the 1949 Motorcycle Show. They were imported models because McCormack and Piaggio needed to test the public's reaction; the receivers, too, needed to be

convinced. McCormack's inspiration had not let him down. The Vespa was the star of the show, with hundreds being ordered on the spot. The press confirmed it - "The Vespa",was they said, " history in the making." McCormack secured from Piaggio the agreement to manufacture the Vespa under licence, and the Receiver gave the go-ahead - Vespa had arrived in the UK.

Naturally there were teething problems. It took much longer than expected to set up machinery and tools, and it was necessary to import certain pressings from Italy. McCormack sensed that most motorcycle dealers would not much care for the Vespa in their showrooms, so he enlisted some enlightened car dealer colleagues for the task. At first, they sold the imported 125, but in March 1951, the Douglas-built Vespa was launched. This Vespa 125, known retrospectively as the 'Rod' model on account of its rod-operated gearchange, was replaced in 1953 by the G model, which had a cable-operated change. Douglas concentrated on building only

Vespas produced under licence by Douglas in Bristol had their headlamps resighted near the top of the apron to meet British regulations.

the Vespa 125 while other models were imported, mainly from the Italian and Spanish factories, although a couple of hundred GSs came in from Germany.

Although the Vespa was much loved and admired in Britain, and the continental style of life it evoked was much sought-after, there was always going to be a problem with sales. For just over half the cost of a Vespa, it was possible to buy a motorcycle of similar capabilities. The Vespa in Britain would never sell itself as a really cheap form of transport as it did in its homeland. Even so, Vespas found favour with several Police forces in England and Ireland, and with the RAC as a convenient working vehicle. They were also much in vogue as the fashionable form of transport for Mods in the 1960s - as epitomised by the film *Quadrophenia*.

By the time production at Kingswood ceased in 1960, over 126,000 units had been built. Douglas continued importing Vespas until 1982, when the franchise was taken over by Vespa (UK) Ltd.

Vespa in Germany

Jacob Oswald Hoffmann was the owner of a bicycle factory in Lintorf, a town just north of Düsseldorf. He had built up the firm himself, having purchased the land and buildings - once the home of a shovel factory - at the end of the war. One day, early in 1949, his attention was caught by some Press photographs of Vespas which had landed on his desk. Here was something fundamentally different - he resolved to find out more. The opportunity came at the Frankfurt Show, where Hoffmann and the Vespa met face to face for the first time. There and then Hoffmann resolved to build the Vespa at Lintorf. He immediately applied to Piaggio for the licence which would enable him to build Vespas for the German market.

Piaggio were extremely pleased to receive Hoffmann's request. They had for some time been watching the German market closely, and were of the firm opinion that Vespas would do very well there. They had made several approaches to likely importers, but had drawn a blank. Delays were kept to a minimum, and the mutually beneficial arrangement was signed and sealed quickly - Hoffmann now owned the exclusive licence to produce Vespas for the whole of West Germany, as well as the right to market Vespas in the northern half of the country, and to export to Holland, Belgium and Denmark. Responsibility for selling to the southern part of the country was assumed by Vespa Marketing GmbH in Frankfurt.

The Vespa quickly became very popular in Germany. Press reports praised its innovation and style, and complimented Piaggio on devising a form of two-wheeled transport with such wide appeal. By 1953, the Hoffmann factory was turning out more than four hundred Vespas per week although,

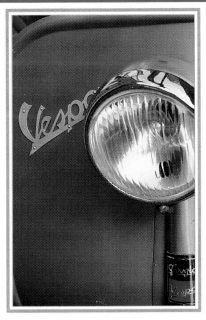

The red and black badge mounted on Vespas that were actually manufactured by Douglas.

within a year, the production rate would fall by half. The economic situation in Germany was not good, but Hoffmann believed he knew the answer; in line with the competition, he would make a Vespa with better performance. This was the Königin model, which was also made to look gutsier by the addition of chromework, an extra headlamp, and so on. The Königin development was costly, and Hoffmann's financial state by then perilous. Making the new scooter also broke the terms of Hoffmann's licence agreement with Piaggio. By the start of 1955, the relationship was over.

Piaggio now formed an alliance with the Messerschmitt company, the first Messerschmitt-Vespa machine rolling off the pro-

duction line in spring 1955. There were to be two models, the 150 *Touren* and the more powerful 150 GS. There was also provision for after sales service and parts for Hoffmann-produced Vespas. This relationship continued until the end of 1957. After this Vespa GmbH Augsburg was established, a company partly owned by Piaggio and partly by the Martial Frane organisation: the latter had previously held a small stake in Vespa-Messerschmitt. The two original models continued to be built, with slight modification over the years, alongside the Vespa 125 which was introduced in 1958. Production continued until 1963, by which time the climate had changed for scooters, and production on a large scale was no longer viable. Thereafter, Vespas were imported into Germany from Italy.

Vespa in France
The first documented sighting of a Vespa on French soil occurred at the Salon de Paris in October 1947. Visitors were fascinated by the new Italian machine proudly displayed on the stand of Georges Monneret. The importing of Vespas into France began in earnest in the spring of 1950 and met with immediate success; in the first nine months, twelve hundred Vespas were sold in France.

In September of 1950, A.C.M.A. (Ateliers de Constructions de Motocycles et Accessories), the headquarters of which was in Paris, took over a factory at Fourchambault, and inherited with it a workforce of 300. They

Douglas only ever manufactured the 125; all the other models they sold were imported from Italy, sometimes from Spain and, exceptionally, from Germany.

immediately set about building Vespa 125s for the French market, with components bought from Italy. The French machines were identical to their Italian cousins in all but one respect - the headlamp had to be mounted on the handlebars to conform with French law.

The popularity of Vespa in France grew apace. By January 1952 ACMA was celebrating the completion of the 10,000th French Vespa. The workforce, now doubled in number to 600, was producing 80 scooters a day. By July, the workers numbered 900, the daily production rate 140. Vespas were sold through a network of 150 dealers throughout France, with 500 further service agents too. The 125 model was joined in 1956 by the 150GL. Based on the 125, bored out to give the extra capacity, the 150GL came with a Zenith carburettor, lockable luggage compartment and white wall tyres.

There had been better years all round for French motorists in general, and scooterists in particular, than 1958. The Suez crisis of the previous year had led to petrol rationing, and there were two increases in tax during the year. Road licences, driving licences and obligatory insurance were all introduced. The only winners were the owners of machines under 50cc, for which restrictions were minimal. Sales of Vespas dropped dramatically.

One of a couple of hundred GSs imported from Germany by Douglas at a time when British demand outstripped Douglas' supply from Italy.

The Piaggio-style Douglas badge on imported Vespas.

Production was slowed, and factory working hours were reduced to 32 per week.

During August the production line was halted altogether.

ACMA introduced versions of both 125 and 150 with narrower body styling and, the following year, supplemented the range with the 150 GS imported from Italy; but the days of Fourchambault were numbered. The factory closed its doors for the last time in 1962; from then on, all Vespas sold in France were imported from Italy by way of Vespa-France. The imported Vespas sold well and the Vespa 50 was able to be more favourably categorised under French law after the addition of pedals (coupled to the rear wheel by means of a chain and independent of the engine). In this form the 50 could legally be driven by anyone over the age of fourteen, with no need for anything so irksome as a driving licence!

There was one other ACMA Vespa, unique and purely practical; the Vespa *Militaire*. In most respects, this Vespa was identical to its 150cc civilian counterpart, although with larger pistons, and reinforcement to assist with the weight it would be required to carry - the prototypes won much praise for their ability to carry 250kg over rough ground. Two versions were produced - TAP 56 and TAP 59 - in the corresponding years.

Opposite: Piaggio had drawn a blank with would-be German importers/manufacturers until, much to their joy, Hoffmann showed a strong interest. Inset: the badge of Hoffmann of Lintorf, near Dusseldorf.

Vespa in Spain

There are many cultural similarities between the Vespa's homeland and Spain, so a good reception was assured. In the early 1950s, Spain was the least-motorised country in Europe; cheap, reliable transport would, therefore, be a boon. From 1952 onwards, Vespas were built under licence by MotoVespa SA in Madrid. Production began slowly, but built up quickly; within four years, 50,000 had rolled off the production line.

The 125 was the first Spanish Vespa, joined in 1959 by the 'S' model, which was equivalent to the *Primavera*, and two years later by the 150. The Vespa 50 S also proved extremely popular with the younger Spanish riders. At the time of writing, MotoVespa SA were still in the Vespa-building business - three basic model groups being produced; the PK, PX and T5/Cosa.

Not such a good idea: the Konigin's altered engine was in breach of Hoffmann's agreement. The model marked the beginning of the end for his relationship with Piaggio. The touring bags are original on this example at the scooter museum at Assmanshausen, Germany.

Vespa GmbH Augsburg produced Vespas until 1963, after which the smoke was Italian in origin.

Vespa in Belgium

Although a few Vespas found their way to Belgium as early as 1949, it was another four years before a proper sales organisation was established by the company of Bevelux in Brussels. They set up a network of 150 sales and service centres throughout Belgium and Luxembourg, as well as selling Vespas through the larger department stores.

From 1954, Vespa 125s were assembled in Belgium by Moto Industry SA (MISA) from parts imported from Italy. From 1956 the range was expanded by the 150 *Tourisme* and 150 GS and, the following year, by

Vespas made by Messerschmitt carried the company's famous flying bird symbol, later the subject of a court case, won by Mercedes!

Small windshields were a popular factory-supplied option but a yellow headlamp was mandatory for France. Inset: ACMA badge.

This ACMA Vespa carries extra fuel in a tank fitted to the spare wheel.

the 150GL. Unfortunately, by the early 1960s, assembly in Belgium was no longer financially viable.

Vespa in the rest of Europe

It is not only in those countries where the Vespa has been built under licence or assembled from imported parts that the Vespa has found fame. One of the first export markets was Switzerland; 60 Vespas crossed the Alps as early as 1946 - the first year of production. Austria, The Netherlands, Denmark, Sweden - consignments of Vespas reached them all.

Vespa in the USA

Piaggio was aware that the United States represented a vast, untapped market for the Vespa. For college students, a decent form of transport they could afford; ideal, too, for farmers; a second 'car' for families; a solution to the problem of getting around traffic-clogged cities.

Sears Roebuck were appointed agents for Vespa in 1951. With little or no promotion, they quickly sold 20,000 Vespa 125s under their own brand name of 'Allstate Cruisaire.' The Vespa's popularity grew rapidly, especially with younger riders and, by the late fifties, this group accounted for well over 90 per cent of the Vespa market.

With its cut-away front (specially shaped to carry a bazooka!) the Military Vespa is certainly one of the most interesting and, some would say, bizarre Vespas.

Advertising accentuated the Vespa's Italianness and the abundance of features, the tag line being 'Power-Safety-Economy.'

Early in 1961, Piaggio struck a deal with scooter manufacturers Cushman, whereby the latter would also sell Vespas in the USA. As Piaggio now had two strings to the Vespa bow in the USA, they also appointed several smaller firms to assist with marketing Vespas in key areas. This period was the Vespa's high point in the USA. In 1975, Piaggio formed the Vespa of America Corporation with an eye to the lucrative Californian market, but met with only limited success. Although there are plenty of enthusiasts in the USA today, Vespas are no longer officially imported.

Vespa in South America
That the Vespa came to be produced under licence in Brazil is due to none other than the legendary racing driver Juan Manuel Fangio. After his retirement from active motor sport, Fangio had made a second career for himself as a successful businessman and entrepreneur, naturally with a keen interest in all things automotive. His factory, Panauto SA, built Vespas throughout the

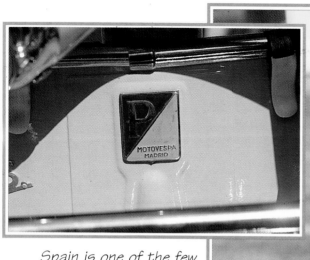

Spain is one of the few countries where Vespas are still produced under licence; this 1959 model is from the early days of Spanish manufacture. Inset: the badge of MotoVespa SA of Madrid.

1950s and '60s, both for Brazil and for export to other South American and Latin American countries. In addition to the public, Vespas found favour with the Brazilian armed forces and with the police.

Vespa in India

In 1961 an agreement was signed between Piaggio and Bajaj Auto Ltd. for the production of Vespas under licence in India. After two years, production moved to a new, large factory in Poona. 150cc Super and *Chetak* models are still produced in India, as well as a 100cc machine called the Cub. Even today the Bajaj scooters are of the old-style Vespa shape. Rugged and dependable, they are ideal for the Indian market where they are very popular.

Bajaj scooters, Vespas built under licence, are ideal transport in India and are, deservedly, very popular. The Chetak 150 shown here is one of three scooters made by Bajaj, the others being the 150cc Super and the 100cc Cub. Inset: The Bajaj badge.

THREE WHEELERS

With the initial success of the Vespa scooter assured, Piaggio developed a three-wheeler based on the scooter, the *APE* (Bee). The first version of APE, known as the model A, was introduced in 1948. At the front end it was identical to its scooter stablemate, while the rear end came in three basic forms - a flat-bed truck, box van or rickshaw-style carrier for two passengers. In practice, of course, the APE was often converted to suit individual owner's needs.

The APE's rider sat on a saddle over the engine, a 125cc unit with four forward gears but no reverse. An add-on windshield was available as an extra, and Piaggio introduced a small cab with open sides for delivery versions, which afforded some weather protection.

The model B APE was introduced in 1955, with a 150cc engine. There were four versions of this model; an open box, either of wood and metal or metal only, a tipper-truck, a closed luggage box and the rickshaw taxi.

At the end of 1956 the model C arrived on the market. The model C APEs had a much more modern appearance and, at last, the driver could be protected by a proper cab. The simplest version comprised a front frame with windshield, but closed-in cabs, with or without doors, were a lot more protective. The traditional saddle was replaced by a small bench seat, which could carry two people - just. A special lever switched the engine into reverse, effectively giving four reverse gears.

There was one special version of the APE, the *Pentaró*, which was introduced in 1961. This came with a 170cc engine, and was effectively a five-wheeled version of the APE. Two years later, the APE model D brought integrated head-lamps, and a completely enclosed cab, with the 170cc engine. In 1965 it was re-designated as model E.

At the start of the 1970s, the APE range - known as 350, 400, 500 & 550 after their load-carrying ability in kilogrammes - was extended by the 250, the 600 and the APE 50, the smallest APE, controlled by means of handlebars rather than a steering wheel. The

Vespa Car made its debut in 1972 marking the move from scooter-based carrier to true light commercial vehicle..

In France, ACMA manufactured their version of the APE, the Tri Vespa, from 1953 to 1958. In excess of 5000 were made in all. Although an APE had appeared on the Douglas show stand alongside the newly imported Vespa scooter, only a few were ever imported into the UK. Bajaj manufactured the APE in India under licence from Piaggio, usually in rickshaw form.

The last twenty years have seen regular updating and redesigning of the APE. In the 1990s the range features over 50 different variations, including eight power units in a choice of petrol, diesel and electric motor forms. In all, more than 1.5 million APEs have been manufactured since this 'working Vespa' was introduced.

On the subject of three-wheeled Vespas, the two-wheeler could be adapted for those who needed to carry extra passengers but for whom the taxi version of the APE was unnecessary. A scooter sidecar was often the solution to the problem of carrying more passengers. There had always been a market for sidecars for motorbikes and there are well-established manufacturers to

La Poste has used APEs in Paris for many years; they don't exactly park in the traditional sense, but they usually manage to stop somewhere without bringing the traffic to a standstill.

The Strasbourg Tourist Department use a variety of APEs and the later Vespa Cars for their round-the-city sightseeing tours . . .
. . . and the Strasbourg Services Department use them to clear up the streets at the end of the day.

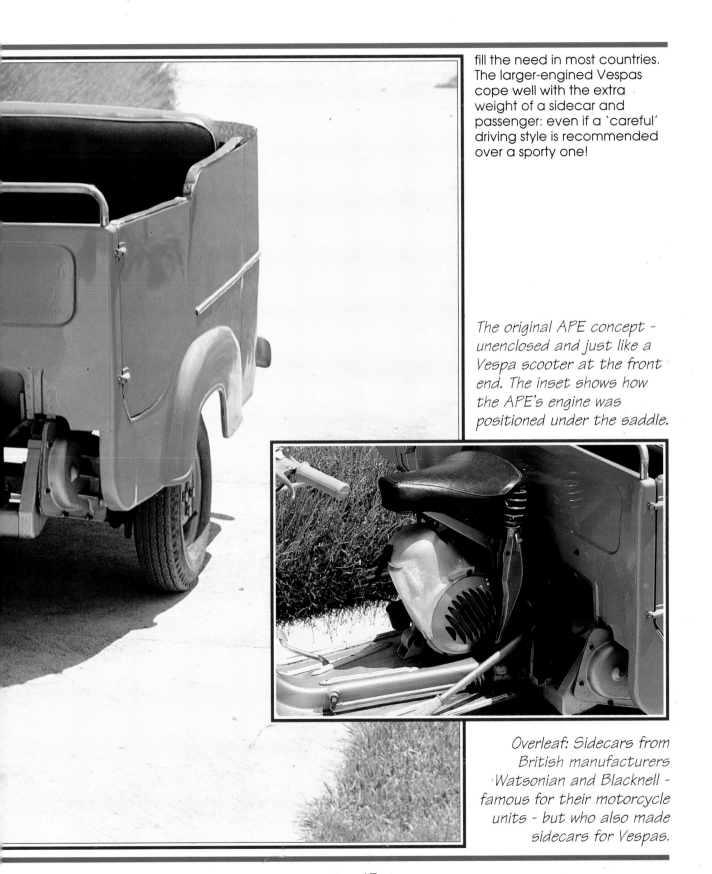

fill the need in most countries. The larger-engined Vespas cope well with the extra weight of a sidecar and passenger: even if a 'careful' driving style is recommended over a sporty one!

The original APE concept - unenclosed and just like a Vespa scooter at the front end. The inset shows how the APE's engine was positioned under the saddle.

Overleaf: Sidecars from British manufacturers Watsonian and Blacknell - famous for their motorcycle units - but who also made sidecars for Vespas.

This older-style sidecar is a Vespa-made unit belonging to a Portuguese enthusiast.

A girl likes to travel in style, and this colour co-ordinated sidecar is just the job.

Two's company - but three need not be a crowd with a stylish sidecar.

5 FOUR WHEELERS

At the Paris Motor Show in October 1957, Vespa unveiled a radical departure from their vehicles' usual two wheels to four - the Vespa 400 car. Piaggio had developed the 400, which was designed by Corradino D'Ascanio, in Italy, but had found themselves in a tricky situation. Fiat, a company of very great influence and in a position to affect Piaggio's supplies of raw materials, took a dim view of an upstart rival to their own newly-announced *Nuova* 500 car. They let it be known that, should Piaggio build Vespa cars in Italy, they would start building scooters. So Piaggio decided to have the 400 built in France at Fourchambault; the cars would carry the ACMA badge.

The Vespa 400 is unusual among the ranks of microcars in that it is, in reality, a scaled-down 'proper' car, rather than a purpose-built micro. The Vespa 400 is very tiny indeed. The interior has tardis-like qualities, though, and there is enough room for two average-sized adults, with plenty of legroom. The handbrake, choke lever and starter lever are situated between

the seats, which restricts passenger room in the middle, but the panels of the doors are hollowed out, which compensates somewhat at each side. The doors are rear-hinged, and more than adequate seat adjustment makes getting in and out easier than it looks.

Although designed to take just two people, plus their luggage, it was possible to buy a cushion for the rear shelf, which converted it into a seat for two children. According to Vespa's own publicity material, the seat would suffice for two 'close friends' - but only on a hot day, as the sunroof would need to be rolled back, and their heads would stick out into the sunshine!

The Vespa's interior is neat and functional, with rubber floor covering and fabric and tubular frame seats. The dashboard is plain and uncluttered, the only instrument being the speedometer with distance recorder and warning lights for indicators, low charge and low fuel. Lights and indicators are operated by stalks and the windscreen wipers by a switch on the

The Vespa 400 is very small - petite and charming, with some very practical features, too.

dash. The standard model has a simple on/off starting switch, the de Luxe model boasts an ignition key. There are switches on the base of the dash for the parking light and, curiously, for reducing the volume of the horn! There is a small recess for maps on the passenger side. Heating and ventilation are rudimentary, but reasonably effective.

The Vespa 400 engine is an air-cooled twin cylinder two-stroke unit of 393cc fitted behind the transaxle. The engine provided 14hp and amazing torque; it could accelerate away from 25km/h (15mph) in top gear. This was made possible by an ingenious system of rotary inlet valves which also allowed very efficient lubrication of the main bearings. A further benefit of this design was the car's ability to run on a petrol/oil mixture of just 50:1, which virtually did away with the

unpleasant blue smoke usually associated with two-stroke power units. The engine is superbly accessible in its rear compartment; to one side is a reservoir for the oil, with a metering device to pump the correct volume of oil into the tank for any quantity of fuel. The gearbox is three-speed plus reverse, with synchromesh on second and third. The 12V battery is mounted on a shelf, which slides out of the nose of

the car. The hydraulic brake fluid reservoir is reached from here, too.

The Vespa 400's top speed was quoted as 90km/h (55mph), this figure featuring as the cruising speed, too. The car is noisy at this speed, but not uncomfortable, thanks to excellent suspension in the French style. A more usual city motoring speed of 70km/h (42mph) is considerably quieter.

The dash is simplicity itself - just the one dial and necessary switches. The front seats are comfortable, in the French manner. The back shelf is designed for luggage, but converts to a rear seat for children with the addition of a cushion which was available as an optional extra.

Having a wheelbase of just under 1.7m and an overall length of just over 2.8m gave the Vespa a tiny turning circle, and made it an excellent car for city driving and parking. Fuel economy confirmed this suitability - (55mpg) under normal driving conditions.

Over 30,000 Vespa 400 cars were built at Fourchambault between 1957 and 1961, by which time production of scooters was also at a low point. During this last year of production, the Vespa 400GT with four-speed gearbox was introduced, although not many were built. A three-speed version with a slightly more powerful engine was manufactured for the export market, and although some 400s found their way to the USA, they never really caught on there. There had been plans to build a right-hand-drive version too, which never came to fruition. The majority of 400s were sold in France or the nearby export markets, in particular Belgium and the Netherlands.

In Europe, there was un-doubtedly potential for the Vespa 400 to become a big success story. It cost a good 20% less than most of the available competitors, yet offered compact size, frugality and reliability. It was neither crude, nor uncomfortable.

Road testing the Vespa

The Vespa 400's doors hinge at the rear, which makes getting in and out straightforward even though the car is so small.

shortly after its introduction the British magazine *Motor* concluded that "... without being in any major fashion unconventional, the Vespa combines ingenious, tested and practical features in a well-integrated whole." The Vespa 400 was a charming car and those that survive today, often lovingly restored and driven, attract attention wherever they go.

With the roof rolled back, two not-too-large adults could make a not-too-long journey in the rear. Inset: Everything in the surprisingly spacious engine compartment is easily to hand. At one time there were rumours that a larger engine might be on the cards, but the bigger unit never materialised.

TWO-WHEELED WONDER

The Vespa scooter was conceived, primarily, as a means of personal transport: the APE being designed as the commercial workhorse Vespa; however, plenty of two-wheelers have worked for their keep and many still do.

The couriers of Paris - either there are thousands of them, or they move around *tres vite* - have found that the Vespa copes well with the horrendous demands of the traffic, the dust, the stop/start nature of the job and the necessity of carrying goods around. Many have screens to protect their riders and some also have side-skirts. Most have boxes, pouches, bags and straps for anchoring the goods.

Many police forces in Europe and South America discovered that the Vespa, though unsuitable for high speed chases and the like, made excellent cheap transport for towns and cities. The Royal Automobile Club of Great Britain owned training Vespas with the capability of being controlled by an instructor sitting at the back, while the student rider learned the steering process and general driving skills.

Vespa motorsport is booming, both on the level of top-class track racing, with all the attendant sponsorship opportunities this brings, and at Vespa club level, with both country- and Europe-wide events well supported and much enjoyed by participants and spectators alike.

In 1960, Douglas supplied the Thames Valley Display Team with two black-painted Vespas. The scooters were slightly modified; reinforcement was necessary so that the various panels could be stood and sat upon with impunity and the gearing was altered to that of a sidecar combination. When Mr. Brian Edwards joined the team in 1962, one of the Vespas was given to him to look after. It was used regularly for displays and practice. After the team gave their last display in 1965, the machines were returned to Douglas, where they were repainted and used as loan machines for club events. Mr. Edwards purchased 'his' original display team Vespa in 1969, using it as daily transport and confining himself to sitting normally on the saddle. He rebuilt the Vespa in the eight-

Mark Green on a Team Vespa 135 machine shows the competition who's boss during a gruelling 150 mile enduro race.

ies, and though it is now decommissioned he still rides it at Vespa rallies and events.

Vespa clubs have been around for almost as long as Vespas; today, clubs are thriving - most weekends in summer will find several Vespa meetings taking place. Regular rallies occur throughout Europe, the annual EuroVespa - hosted by a different country each year - being the highspot of the calendar.

Of course, there are those

Andrew Merchant on a Quartz 70 during a race for automatics up to 70cc only.

Some competition can be less intense than racing round a track, but muddier. It's possible to slip and slide all over the place and still hang on, but there is a point of no return! This mud-bath courtesy of the Vespa Club Dusseldorf.

for whom their Vespa is just a means of transport but there are many, many, enthusiasts for whom it represents a way of life. For such enthusiasts, the Vespa has ceased to be merely a means to an end and has become an end in itself.

A Paris courier's Cosa, with leather skirt for weather protection. The ideal machine for weaving in and out of traffic jams . . .

. . . and even if your hometown is less frantic than Paris, a Vespa makes an excellent workhorse.

Gerona traffic police cruise the strada on their regulation white Vespas.

Opposite: Vespas certainly get around - some of them extremely heavily laden, as this Swiss example, photographed in Hampshire, England, shows.

With two-wheeled transport, the feeling of being in tune with your surroundings is heightened, and is the main reason why scooter enthusiasts leave the car at home.

This French ACMA Vespa is a television star - it appeared in an episode of the Granada TV production of Maigret alongside the Inspector's famous Citroen Traction Avant car.

Owners spend serious time and money on their Vespas - and the finished result is worth the effort. Inspiration can come from pop culture, films, cartoons, news stories and, in this case, Jaguar's Le Mans team livery.

Brian Edwards' ex-Thames Valley Display Team Vespa, its paintwork restored to the black of its performing days.

Vespa clubs are booming - the annual EuroVespa is an ideal opportunity for owners from many countries to get together and talk Vespa.

SCOOTER STYLE 7

A Vespa is a personal thing - no two people look exactly alike, think exactly alike, act exactly alike - and no two Vespas are exactly alike either. So everyone will respond to their Vespa differently as the pictures in this chapter show.

Photographer's Postscript

I hope you have enjoyed the photographs in this book.

The joy of two-wheeled subjects, from a photographer's point of view, is that there are many more locations available - locations which are inaccessible to four-wheelers. Sometimes, especially for the owners, this freedom brings problems. The picture on page 17 is a good example. There are hundreds of steps leading to the Cathe-dral in Gerona and I wanted to picture a Vespa half way up those steps . . . When Oliver Körber heard me make the request to the owner of a much-chromed machine and the negative response I got, he immediately offered his own machine and a 'lifting party' to get it into position. After all this effort, we were rather bemused to see the yellow Vespa immediately surrounded by photographers!

My special thanks to Oliver for this effort, and his unstinted help in Aix and his home town of Landau.

In all these endeavours, my constant companions have been my Leica R6 cameras and a range of lenses from 16mm to 400mm. The pictures in this book were all produced on Fujichrome film.

David Sparrow

Dear Reader,
We hope you enjoyed this Veloce Publishing production. If you have ideas for other books on Vespa, or
other marques, please write and tell us.
Meantime, Happy Scootering!